The Gift of Prayer

Strengthening Community Wellbeing

**Sherrye Willis &
Alliance for Greater Works™**

Foreword By Dr. Cynthia Rembert James

Cocoon to Wings
PUBLISHING

THE GIFT OF PRAYER
Copyright © 2025 Alliance for Greater Works

All rights reserved. This book or any portion thereof may not be reproduced, distributed, or transmitted in any form or by any means, including photocopying, recording, or other electronic or mechanical methods, without the express written permission of the publisher except in the case of brief quotations embodied in critical reviews and certain other noncommercial uses permitted by copyright law. For permissions requests, write to the publisher, addressed "Attention: Permissions Coordinator," at the address below.

Printed in the United States of America
ISBN: 978-1-963964-26-4 (Hardcover)

Published by Cocoon to Wings Publishing
7810 Gall Blvd., #311
Zephyrhills, FL 33541
www.CocoontoWingsBooks.com
(813) 906-WING (9464)

Scriptures marked KJV are taken from the HOLY BIBLE, KING JAMES VERSION (KJV): KING JAMES VERSION, public domain.
Scriptures marked NIV are taken from the HOLY BIBLE, NEW INTERNATIONAL VERSION® (NIV®): Copyright ©1973, 1978, 1984, 2011 by Biblica, Inc.® Used by permission. All rights reserved worldwide.

The Gift of Prayer

A GIFT

TO: ....

FROM: ....

MESSAGE: ....

....

....

....

....

....

....

TABLE OF CONTENTS

Foreword	xi
Preface	xiii
Prayers For Alliance For Greater Works	1
Prayers for those served by Alliance for Greater Works	3
Prayers for the Future of Alliance	7
A Prayer for the Church of Jesus Christ	11
A Prayer for Salvation	13
A Prayer for Children	15
Prayers for Godly Friends	17

Prayers for Families	19
A Prayer for Young People to Honor Their Parents and Others	21
A Prayer for Teens	23
Prayers for Schools and Educators	25
A Prayer for High School and College Students	29
A Prayer for Good Health	31
A Prayer for All People	33
A Prayer for Safety and Protection	35
A Prayer for the Graduates	37
A Prayer to End Gun Violence	39
A Prayer for the Mental Health of our Country	41
A Prayer for the Mental Health Professionals	43
A Prayer for the Mental Health Stakeholders	45
A Prayer for Healing, Restoration, and Good Health	47

A Prayer for Caregivers	49
A Prayer for First Responders	51
A Prayer for Parents	53
A Prayer for Law Enforcement	55
Prayers for Legislators	57
Prayers for Community Healing	61
A Prayer for Obedience to His Direction	63
A Prayer for the Nation	65
A Prayer for Families and Communities	67
A Prayer for Times of Crisis & Suffering	69
A Prayer for Global Peace and Stability	71
A Prayer for Justice & Righteousness	73
A Prayer for the Economy & Workforce	75
A Prayer for Mental & Emotional Well-being	77

A Prayer for the Military & Veterans	79
Prayers for the Vulnerable and the Oppressed	81
A Prayer for the Persecuted Church	83
A Prayer for the Next Generation	85
A Prayer to Breathe Life into Our Communities, Nation, and the World	87
The Gift of Prayer Book Contributors	93
Special Thanks	96

FOREWORD

Prayer is both an intimate conversation with God and a divine summons to stand in the gap for our world. When I was called to lead this prayer for the National Day of Prayer, my heart was heavy with the needs of nations, communities, and families. Yet, I prayed with confidence because the same God who begins a good work in us is faithful to complete it.

I prayed for peace. Not the fragile peace of politics or policies, but the eternal peace that flows from the heart of God. A peace that can heal nations, quiet wars, and restore justice where injustice cries out. A peace that embraces children who are hungry, families who are displaced, and those silenced by poverty or oppression.

I prayed for leaders. Not merely leaders of influence, but leaders of courage, ablaze with faith, alive in spirit, and committed to creating communities of grace in the midst of chaos. Leaders who will gather children at the borders, speak for the poor, care for the sick, and love the forgotten. Leaders who will refuse to settle for material gain or empty prestige, but instead live authentically, making the gospel real in every sphere of life.

I prayed for justice. For the millions held in conflict zones, for the children denied education, for prisoners without hope of release, for those whose lives are taken by violence every seven minutes around the world. Our cry for justice is also a cry for mercy, for God to forgive us where our systems have failed, where privilege has silenced compassion, and where prejudice has divided us.

And I prayed for the next generation. A generation unafraid to dream, to act, and to believe that God is still moving in the earth. A generation that refuses to dwell in the past but embraces the mystery of His presence in the now. A generation of fire-carriers who will bring hope, truth, and transformation.

The Gift of Prayer is a reminder that prayer is not passive. It is action. It is resistance against despair, silence against prejudice, and healing against brokenness. Prayer fuels us to believe that even in ashes, God stirs the embers of a new tomorrow.

May this book awaken in you the urgency to pray, not only for yourself, but for the world God so loves. May it stir your spirit to intercede for peace, justice, and authentic leadership. And may it remind you, as it has reminded me, that prayer is God's invitation to partner with Him in His redemptive work in the earth.

To Him be glory forever and ever. Amen.

Dr. Cynthia Rembert James
Landmark Ministries & Protege

PREFACE

Since 2020, our world has faced one crisis after another: a global pandemic, economic strain, rising violence, and increasing mental health challenges. In such seasons, we are left asking: What do we do when the world feels like it's unraveling? Where can we turn when human strength is not enough?

The answer is prayer, prayer to a living God who invites us to cast our cares on Him (1 Peter 5:7). Intercessory prayer, in particular, offers far more than comfort; it invites God's power into situations beyond our control. Research even confirms what believers have long known: prayer benefits both the one being prayed for and the one praying, fostering emotional, spiritual, and even physical wellbeing.

This book was inspired by One Hour of Prayer, an annual gathering hosted by Alliance for Greater Works™ in observance of the National Day of Prayer and Mental Health Awareness Month. Since 2020, leaders, neighbors, and friends from all walks of life have united to seek God's face for the wellbeing of our communities, nation, and world. Many have returned year after year, sharing how that single hour brought hope, peace, and renewed strength.

In celebration of Alliance's 25th anniversary, we wanted to give that same gift of prayer in a lasting form. *The Gift of Prayer* brings together 50 heartfelt prayers from a diverse group of voices, board members, program partners, friends, and churches from our Resilient Church Collective (RCC). The RCC equips and mobilizes congregations across Texas (and beyond) to respond to the trauma caused by COVID-19, intergenerational wounds, and community violence. Proceeds from this book will help strengthen that mission.

For more than 25 years, Alliance has served people of every background, committed to a vision where all individuals can thrive, regardless of zip code. We believe prayer is not a last resort, but a first line of action, and when God's people pray, communities flourish.

May these prayers draw you closer to God's heart and inspire you to lift your voice for the wellbeing of others, knowing that your prayers matter more than you may ever realize.

Sherrye Willis
Founder and President
Alliance for Greater Works™

PRAYERS FOR ALLIANCE FOR GREATER WORKS

Dr. Maurice Pugh

Dear Father, thank You for Your faithfulness to this ministry. Thank You for Sherrye and Joe Willis and their team. Thank You for their mission and vision to equip and train leaders to maximize their Kingdom purpose, while bringing social and systemic change to neighborhoods and communities.

Father, give them fresh and bold clarity as they continue to chart new ground and go into new places courageously with bold strategies. May they continue to equip and strengthen organizations and ministries to do the work that You have called them to do.

We pray, Father, for ongoing financial support and that You continue to show Yourself faithful financially. We pray for Your favor, knowing that as Your hand is upon them, greater works they will continue to do. We pray that countless ministries, organizations, and leaders will thrive as a result of their experience and training.

Father, I thank You for the word 'alliance,' which means partnership. We are partnering to help others fulfill what You've called them to do. And we thank You for greater works, because even Your Son says greater works we shall do. We pray, Father, that You continue to be glorified through our efforts and work in Your Son's name. Amen.

Jeff Howard

God, we come before you today with one agenda and one purpose: to seek Your face and pray for Your blessing, will, and purpose for Alliance for Greater Works. God, thank You for allowing this nonprofit to represent every part of this nation and to help people of every background. And we stand before the Almighty, who transcends politics, moves mountains and men, and before whom kingdoms and kings rise and fall, nations ascend and descend before him, who changes not, but He remains the same yesterday, today, and forever. We come before You, before whom men and women, peoples and nations have come from ages past. We come before You to seek Your face in these uncertain and challenging times as we pray for community healing, pray for those served by the Alliance, and pray for our future. In Jesus' name. Amen.

PRAYERS FOR THOSE SERVED BY ALLIANCE FOR GREATER WORKS

Elaine Sommerville

Our God, our Redeemer, Your Word from Galatians 6:2, tells us, "Bear one another's burdens, and so fulfill the law of Christ."

Lord, we bring to You all the ministry and nonprofit leaders who have interacted with Alliance and will continue to do so. We pray for the leaders of these nonprofits and these ministries that You would give them strength and renewal after a season of weariness has been upon them. Father, strengthen them for the tasks before them. We pray that You open their hearts and minds to embrace the wisdom, knowledge, and guidance that the Alliance brings.

And, Father, we ask that You refresh all their ministries and organizations, and that You provide for them supernaturally. Open their eyes to see the needs of their communities, give them fresh revelation to know where the hurt and need are, and where their attention needs to go.

Lord, we pray that You continue to show Alliance great favor so that the seeds planted today not only bring current changes but also provide a great harvest for the Kingdom over the years to come. In the mighty name of Jesus, we pray. Amen.

Frank Sommerville

Father God, we bow before You in prayer. You are the Lord of marginalized communities. You know what it's like to be in a community that has been set aside, that has been discriminated against, and that experiences violence. Lord, You are in these marginalized communities today. You see the hardships and the barriers that prevent them from experiencing life in full. You see all things. You have called Alliance to bear their burdens. You have called Alliance to shine the spotlight on their plight, on their problems, and on their barriers.

We pray that youth and families in these communities will recognize their need for You. We pray that they will recognize their need for Alliance's services and the programs that show them a way out of their wilderness. We pray that You would anoint Alliance as they present solutions regardless of race, color, or economic status. They will then be able to instruct and share the wisdom, knowledge, and understanding they have gained to help Your people. We ask You to open the doors for alliances, and that You transform lives through the power of prayer and through the power of community. We pray that burdens be lifted and that communities feel refreshed and energized to continue (or begin) to serve You, oh Lord. We submit these words to You, in Your Son's holy name. Amen.

PRAYERS FOR THE FUTURE OF ALLIANCE

Dr. David Wang

Lord, according to Your Word, we thank You for Your persistent faithfulness, guidance, leading, and provision to Alliance and to all who are leading it. We look forward to the future with confidence because it is You who started this good work at Alliance.

Lord, accordingly, we pray over all of those who have been blessed by the programs and initiatives of Alliance. We pray for all those who will be involved in the future initiatives. We pray for the next generation of leaders who will lead our country, our communities, our denominations, and our churches. We pray that we will be faithful stewards. We acknowledge that You bear witness to the many forms of hidden violence, hidden physical pain, and hidden emotional and psychological pain that our youth quietly bear. We pray that this hidden pain is not a source of long-term destruction and distraction, nor that it causes them to stray from their holy calling. We pray that for more years to come, we might be Your hands and feet, that we might be a channel, a conduit through which Your love, comfort, and healing can be freely given and administered. We pray for all of these things, even as people who still carry our own pain as well. We pray that You empower all of us to be repairers of the breach. We pray that Your coming ordained leaders might complete this work in even greater intimacy with You. In Jesus' name we pray. Amen.

LaLoni Leffall

Everything in the heavens and earth is Yours, oh Lord. This is Your Kingdom, and we stand in adoration. We honor You because You control all things with power and might. We pray that we will be sensitive to the Holy Spirit's call to be used by You. And Father, just like You multiplied the five loaves and the two fish to feed the multitude of people, we pray that You multiply our impact in the Kingdom of God. We need the power and presence of Your Holy Spirit to do the work You have called us to do. Help us to know what You have uniquely called each one of us to do.

Father, we are very aware that when we set out to do great work, we will be met by spiritual warfare. So, we pray that we will be equipped, wearing the full armor of God. We will put it on from our head to our feet. God, we pray that You forgive us for any time that we have neglected to respond to the promptings of the Holy Spirit. We pray that today be the day we respond with boldness to Your prompting to serve You well.

Father, we ask that You give us clarity about where You want us to serve. And that we declare, like Isaiah did with the invitation to do Your work, "Here am I. Send me." Father, we honor and praise You. In Jesus Christ's name and to God be the glory. Amen.

A PRAYER FOR THE CHURCH OF JESUS CHRIST

Dr. Ricky Walter

Father, we pray for the body of Christ today. We pray that we conduct our lives in a manner worthy of You, bearing fruit in every good work and steadily growing and increasing in You. Reinvigorate and strengthen us according to Your glory. Father, thank You for qualifying us to share in the portion that is our inheritance. Thank You for delivering and transforming us, moving us from the dominion of darkness.

We pray that we become more aware of what You desire from us. We pray that the division in the body of Christ be erased. Amass Your people to stand on the word of the Lord. We pray that You crush every weapon that is formed against pastors and leaders. Grant them the spirit of Solomon, to lead with sound wisdom, knowledge, and understanding. Lead them with the Holy Spirit.

And Father, whatever pastors are going through, whether physical, mental, or emotional, grant them healing. We thank You for being the One who provides joy. Father, give Your people who are discouraged joy. And let that joy become strength. In the midst of challenges, help them to push through and to stand true to their calling. Lord, our walk is determined. We're steadfast. We endure because Your Word says we can. Father, we trust You. Help us to lay aside every weight that impedes the things that You have called us to do. This we ask You in Jesus' name. Amen.

A PRAYER FOR SALVATION

Pastor Annie Nelson

Father, we give Your name praise, glory, and honor, and we thank You for allowing us the privilege and the opportunity to come into Your presence. Lord, we come before You, asking for Your Spirit in our lives. We pray for the gift of Your salvation. We pray for Your awesome offering of grace that not only promises us eternal life but also gives us the divine ability to live our daily lives with Your presence. We thank You for the ability to walk with You, talk with You, and be led by You. God, You are our new government. Father, we ask for this presence in our lives. We not only ask for Your eternal renewal and change of heart, but a right now change in our spirits, our souls, our hearts, and our minds. Renew us, by Your power, oh God. Recreate us to be the image of the living Jesus Christ, being pleasing in Your sight in every way, every day. Change us, oh God, that we be like unto You. In the name of Jesus, we pray. Amen.

If you desire to welcome Jesus into your heart as Savior, read these words aloud. "Father, I believe in my heart that You are the one and only God. You manifested Yourself as Jesus Christ, our Savior. I know that Jesus died for my sins, that He rose again, and now sits at the right hand of God. He has forgiven and corrected any sins in my life through His death, and I believe that I am made whole, no matter my mistakes. I believe this by faith through Your grace. You said, if I believe and I receive this truth, that I am saved. Lord, I thank You for saving my spirit, my soul, and my body, and calling me Your child, in Jesus' name, I pray. Amen."

A PRAYER FOR CHILDREN

Rylee Vlaun-Wright

Our Father in heaven, thank You for being a good Father. Thank You for life and loving us. Thank You for protecting children like me around the world. Give us a spirit that will make us wise in Your knowledge and give us a great understanding of Your heart. Father, let us know the hope You have given us, as Your rich blessings. Remind us that You have promised Your great power to all who believe. Thank You, in Jesus' name. Amen.

PRAYERS FOR GODLY FRIENDS

Brennan Timm

Thank You, God, for the opportunity to come to You about Godly friends. We know it was important to You because You had twelve close friends (disciples). In John 15:12-13, You said, "My command is this: greater love has no one than this: to lay down one's life for a friend." Thank You for all the people You have brought into our lives who are Godly. Help us to find more people who are looking for You. Help us to be the friends that You have called us to be. Help us to be kind, patient, and caring to those You'll bring to us in the future. We trust You to do great things. In Jesus' name we pray. Amen.

Bryce Timm

Dear God, thank You for putting specific people in our lives. Thank You for giving us God-centered friends to talk to about anything that we're struggling with and anything that we need help with. Thank You for relationships with people who are God-centered, with whom we can openly talk to about You. Thank You for also allowing us to be a representative of You by being there to help out when needed. We appreciate You for bringing all these types of people into our lives, and we pray that they be with us for a very long time. In Jesus' name we pray. Amen.

PRAYERS FOR FAMILIES

K. Graham

Dear God, we pray for our families. What we want most is for You to give us the will and strength to stick together even through rough times. Whenever we walk into a room and our family is there, let our face glow with happiness. May we love and honor the special moments we share, and we pray that those last. We pray for the families that are homeless. We pray that they are safe with shelter, food, and water. Dear Lord, please give them strength and hope along their journey. Lastly, we pray for families that are in countries of war. Please give them the strength to believe in You, that You can do miraculous things. We love You. In Jesus' name. Amen.

Pastor Vincent Parker

Father, it is a privilege to come before Your throne and Your presence. We come to lift families to You. You are the designer of families of all kinds, including those who walked through the trauma of divorce, abuse, challenges, distraction, delay, and difficult seasons. We pray that You would provide, open up doors, and open the windows of heaven and pour out blessings. God, you have incarnated Yourself among us, so you know intimately what each family needs. I pray that You would meet each one at that point of need. Provide, heal, and comfort. But even more so, Father, we pray that those things hindering the joy You designed life to provide are removed. We pray that each family would experience every joy, every blessing, every hope, every dream, and every experience You have in store for them. Continue to be the Father that families need, being present in each moment. May Your Holy Spirit be a comforter, guide, director, and source of ever-needed joy. We ask these things in Your Son's name according to the authority that You have given to us through the blood of Jesus Christ. Amen.

A PRAYER FOR YOUNG PEOPLE TO HONOR THEIR PARENTS AND OTHERS

Jacob Garcia

Lord God, we come to You today so thankful for who You are. For You are Jehovah Jireh, You're Jehovah Nissi. You are El Shaddai. And God, we give You praise for You are a mighty fortress. God, we come on behalf of children. We pray that they will be obedient to their parents as Your Word commands. We pray that they do not stray away from the teaching and the instruction of their parents, but that they listen to them. God, give them a heart of repentance. Turn their eyes toward You so that they would do exactly what You have set them to do. Lord God, we honor You. We give You glory. It's in the mighty name of Jesus that we pray. Amen.

A PRAYER FOR TEENS

Vivian Jackson

Dear Lord, thank You for this day and for all the wonders of our amazing world. Sometimes kids don't see the wonders. They see darkness and feel sad. We come to You with the insecurities of teenagers on our hearts. They are concerned about their looks, their grades, their futures, and how others view them. Their peers have witnessed some, like me, being bullied for various reasons. Things like gossip, rumors, and accusations fly around our schools and communities, threatening people's reputations. Young people often feel hopeless, scared, worried, and unsure of themselves. We become depressed and have a hard time experiencing joy and feeling loved.

Sometimes teens feel alone and misunderstood. Sometimes those feelings, and the enemy, lead them to want to hurt themselves or others. Maybe they think drugs or alcohol will help. We ask You to help us overcome these struggles and difficulties. Give peace of mind to youth of all ages, including those who are bullying others. Let them know that You are with them through everything and that You will not leave them. Lord, please give the adults in our lives a better understanding of the challenges we face. Lord, please help us not to keep our concerns to ourselves. Give us the strength to tell them what worries us, just as we tell You. We ask that You continue to watch over us, and please guide us so that we may help others along the way. Thank You, Lord. Amen.

PRAYERS FOR SCHOOLS AND EDUCATORS

Grayland Barrett

God, we come bowed down, asking that You bless the schools and educators. Bless those who are unable to attend school; those who are suffering, who are going through different trials and tribulations in their lives. God, as they go to school and try to make something out of themselves for their families, we ask You to touch all the children. God, we ask You to touch the adults. Keep them safe. Put Your arms of protection around them. Put Your love around them. Put Your hedge of protection around them. We ask for Your continuous abundance, God of love, of grace, and of mercy. We ask for Your continuous abundance, coming down on us. We continually thank You for it all, all You have done, and all You continue to do. In Jesus' name I pray. Amen.

Elder Melvin Lee

Holy Spirit, we pray for You to be with teachers who are responsible for our children's education. Put Your righteousness in their hearts, and Your words on their lips. So that they may share them with Your children in their daily work. Lord, we pray for the educators and administrators. We understand that they have families and lives. Many are stressed out by the testing and daily assignments. We are praying for their strength, praying for their families. Lord, no weapon formed against them shall prosper. We're praying for safety and security over our schools. No weapon formed against the schools shall prosper. No hurt, harm, or danger will come nigh according to Psalm 91. Lord, we ask that You continue to encamp Your arms around educators, administrators, and every staff member. Be a shield of protection. We plead the blood of Jesus over our schools and educators. I pray that educators will continue to breathe life into our scholars and give them new mindsets, letting them know that they have value. Lord God Almighty, we pray these things in Jesus' name. Amen.

Dr. Cynthia McKnight

Heavenly Father, You are the giver of all wisdom and knowledge. We come before You with grateful hearts, lifting every student, teacher, and administrator who walks the halls of learning. Lord, let each child know that they are fearfully and wonderfully made according to Psalms 139:14.

Father, kindle their curiosity, sharpen their minds, and tender their hearts. Where there is anxiety, replace it with Your perfect peace. Guard their identity in Christ so that their light will shine in this dark world. Surround them with individuals, mentors, and friendships who will encourage and nurture righteousness and speak life into and concerning them.

We pray that You anoint the educators with Your spirit of wisdom and understanding. Renew their strength daily as they soar on wings like eagles, so they do not grow weary. Fill their mouths with gracious words seasoned with salt. That they will build up each learner. Reward their unseen labor and let the work of their hands be established. May they teach not merely from textbooks, but from their heart that is anchored in Your truth and with Your love.

Father, we pray that you guide the administrative staff and order their footsteps. Grant the principals and counselors Your peace, insight, and support. Bless them with courage, justice, and compassion, as You shepherd them. Let Your integrity and excellence shine in all they do.

Break down every barrier of inequity and open doors of opportunity. Send Your angels to encamp around them. We seal this prayer in the mighty, matchless name of Jesus. It is so, and so shall it be according to thy Word. Amen.

A PRAYER FOR HIGH SCHOOL AND COLLEGE STUDENTS

Lanai Johnson

Father, as we come before Your throne, we stand on Your Word in Proverbs 3:5-6. "Trust in the Lord with all Your heart and lean not on Your own understanding; in all Your ways submit to him, and he will make Your paths straight." Dear Lord, please bless those who are navigating the halls of high school and college. Grant them the strength to rise above their challenges, the wisdom to discern their paths, and the courage to pursue their dreams unapologetically. Give them the power to embrace their heritage and stand tall in their identity, walking confidently in their purpose. Surround them with mentors who understand their journey, friends who will uplift their spirits, and opportunities that will propel them forward. As they journey through life's twists and turns, may they hear Your voice, feel Your hand guiding them, and know Your love is sustaining them. These and other blessings we ask in Jesus' name. Amen.

A PRAYER FOR GOOD HEALTH

Jada Jones

Heavenly Father, thank You for health. We pray for continued good health for all. Lord, please heal all those who are sick. Keep us safe from injuries to our bodies, minds, and souls. Give us good health and energy so that we can serve You and serve our friends, families, and communities. Lord, protect us from sickness and disease. Lord, give us strength. In Jesus' name we pray. Amen.

A PRAYER FOR ALL PEOPLE

Kierston Harris

Father God, we come to You, thanking You for everyone reading these words. Thanking You for everything that You have done, everything that You're doing now, and everything that You're going to do. We come to You, God, asking for peace, stability, and help. Give us grace in this time, because this world is crazy, and we don't know what everyone is battling with. We don't know what everyone's dealing with. But we come to You, God, asking for grace for them, for me, for all of us.

Give us grace to know that we may make mistakes, and we may do things that are not like You or of You, Father God, but we ask for grace and forgiveness. We ask for mental encouragement for those who are battling demons mentally and emotionally. Father, let them know that no matter what they're dealing with, You will always be there. That You are always with them, Lord Jesus. That You are always by their side. It may not feel like it, but let them know that You are always there, and that no matter what, they can lean on, call on, and talk to You. Let them know that everything will be okay.

Father, let them understand that it may be hard right now, but it's only a season. Give them the peace that they need. Give them the hug that they need. God, allow someone to speak life into them today. Give us the right words to say and the right things to do, so that we can be a blessing or help to them. We come to You, saying thank You, Father God. Thank You for that understanding, peace, and reminders that You're always going to be there. We love You and we thank You, God. We may not feel it, but we know that You are there. Let us remember, even in those times of being unfaithful, Father God, You give us the faith that we need to make it. In Jesus' name we pray. Amen.

A PRAYER FOR SAFETY AND PROTECTION

Brandon Sanders

Dear Father God, we come, once again, just to thank You. Thank You for allowing us to wake up and see another day. Father, we ask for Your safety and protection. We know this is a cruel world, and a lot of things are happening. But we look to You, for You are our help in the middle of battle. We're asking that You keep Your arms and Your hands around us, Father. As we continue to move through this world. Father God, we thank You for giving Your only begotten Son who hung, bled, and died so we have the right to the Tree of Life. In Jesus' name. Amen.

A PRAYER FOR THE GRADUATES

Madison Brown

Dear Heavenly Father, we pray that You bless graduates on every educational level. May they continue to challenge themselves intellectually and share the fruits of their knowledge to make a positive difference in the world You created. Lord, we ask that You surround graduates to grow with Your wisdom and grace. Bless them with hope so that they can move into futures with eager and open hearts. In Jesus' name we pray. Amen.

A PRAYER TO END GUN VIOLENCE

Dr. Sheron Patterson

God of the slain, God of the murderer, God of the victim. Attend to our prayers today. Our hearts are broken with the pain and the senseless deaths caused by gun violence. We mourn. We live in fear. We do not feel safe anywhere. The doctor's office, the school, the grocery store, the movies, or at home. We ask that You touch our nation with Your love, heal our brokenness, and turn us away from violence toward peace. That our hands reach out and connect with those who feel alone, and those suffering from a mental illness. Let our voices be raised, beseeching our legislators to enact gun laws to protect all in our society, especially those most vulnerable. Let our pens write messages demanding change while also scripting words of hope and transformation. We ask this in the name of God, who desires that we live together in peace. Amen.

A PRAYER FOR THE MENTAL HEALTH OF OUR COUNTRY

Minister Leonard Allen

Lord God, we ask You, in Jesus' name, to protect our country from all evil, hurt, harm, and dangers seen and unseen. Teach us Your Words so that we may love and understand those among us with mental health challenges. Bless us to walk in excellent health and to grow in grace and knowledge that we may come together in strength and wisdom.

Bless each of us to have and always seek to have an ever-growing, closer walk and stronger relationship with Thee. May that relationship develop a deeper companionship and understanding of the trauma and impact that mental health has on our country. Bless us all to have a God-solution-focused heart, mind, spirit, and attitude that will lead us to engage in healing activities for the country. May we each day have a heart of forgiveness, thanksgiving, and gratitude for who You are and all that You have done and will do in our lives.

Restore our brokenness with healing love. We speak life, reform, peace, justice, unity, stability, to our country. God, we lay our fear and anxiety at Your feet. We ask that You help us overcome all our doubts and fears. Remind us that You are an all-powerful God. Remind us that we can trust You. We cannot do anything on our own, but through You, all things are possible. In Jesus' name. Amen.

A PRAYER FOR THE MENTAL HEALTH PROFESSIONALS

Dr. Erica Holmes

Our gracious God and loving Father, we offer a prayer of thanksgiving and support for mental health professionals, psychologists, and psychiatrists, for marriage and family therapists, for licensed professional counselors, licensed clinical social workers, and all other mental health therapists and service providers. Lord, we praise You for all the ways that You have equipped them with the skills needed to perform the work that You have purposed for them to do.

Lord, we pray that those they encounter through their work experience Your reflection, Your grace, Your compassion, Your mercy, Your comfort, and Your hope as they struggle through trying times. Protect the minds of mental health professionals and their very souls. We pray that You fill them with Your Holy Spirit and strength. Help empower them to do Your work.

Remind them of Your presence, God, that in times of isolation, they are not alone, and You are near them.

Give them praise in their hearts for the heavy burdens that they carry for others. And as they experience the woes of life themselves while they help others, Lord, we ask for Your comfort. Bring someone to walk alongside mental health professionals, Lord, to continually pray for them and to encourage them. And, when they feel overwhelmed, comfort and strengthen them. When they feel like they aren't making a difference, refresh their sense of purpose and the call that You have placed on their life, oh God. And give them rest and renewal in You, guide them as they lead others, and show them Your hope. May they be met with a cheerful heart and kind word from everyone they encounter. Jesus, it is in Your holy and matchless name, we pray. Amen.

A PRAYER FOR THE MENTAL HEALTH STAKEHOLDERS

Vicky Coffee

Heavenly Father, thank You for Your Word, which says that we should pray without ceasing. Lord, Your children are hurting spiritually, emotionally, and physically. We pray for their healing and remind them that You will never leave us or forsake us, even in our times of trouble.

God, we come to You on behalf of those who are blessed with the opportunity to direct funding to people, individuals, families, and communities in need of mental health services. Matthew 25:40 (NIV) says, "Truly I tell you, whatever you did for one of the least of these brothers and sisters of mine, you did for me."

Lord, help them remember that they can improve the lives of our brothers and sisters who are vulnerable, those who are socially, psychologically, or economically disadvantaged. Guide those in decision-making roles, Lord. Help them to be fair, equitable, and inclusive in supporting all communities. Help them select organizations that have the right mission, the right vision, and the right heart for serving Your people. You are the Creator of opportunities and all things, including the funds, come from You. We ask that You keep them humble and mindful that it is a privilege to help others. And more importantly, that their position has been gifted by You.

God, thank You for Your grace, mercy, and guidance. In Jesus' name. Amen.

A PRAYER FOR HEALING, RESTORATION, AND GOOD HEALTH

Pastor Tonya McGill

Father, in the name of Jesus, we come to You today praying for healing, restoration, and good health across this land. Second Chronicles 7:14 declares that, if Your people who are called by Your name will humble themselves and pray and seek Your face and turn from their wicked ways, then You will hear from heaven and You will forgive our sin and heal our land. We stand on this promise today. We come humbly before You, praying and seeking Your face. We repent for our sins. Therefore, we believe that You are hearing from heaven, forgiving our sin, and healing our land.

We pray that You would heal us from every sickness and every disease. We pray that You would supernaturally heal our bodies, heal our minds, and even heal our souls. We ask for Your healing over every part of our lives, physically, emotionally, mentally, and spiritually. We ask You to heal our land. We ask You to make us whole, to restore our health, and to heal our wounds. We ask that You make us strong as we draw near to You. We pray that we will prosper and be in good health, even as our soul prospers. We ask for Your divine intervention of healing throughout this land. We lean fully upon You, Lord, for You alone are able. Thank You for Your grace that helps us and strengthens us. We love You, Lord, and we agree with Your Word and Your promises, and we ask these things, humbly in the name of Jesus. Amen.

A PRAYER FOR CAREGIVERS

Pastor Anita Jahwar

Father, we come to ask that You touch every person who serves as a caregiver. Lord, we ask that they walk with You throughout the day. We pray that they won't experience burnout. Give them the peace that surpasses all understanding, as they make various decisions.

Father, we thank You for tranquility and for walking with them. No matter whom they are caring for, let them discern Your peace and Your will. As they take care of others, Lord, allow them to do it with a Christ-like love at all times, even in times of pressure, drama, sickness, or separation.

Give them divine understanding. In every situation that may arise, bless their thoughts, their attitudes, and their well-being. We pray that they will have blessed sleep. Cover them right now from the top of their head down to the soles of their feet, Father God. Give them the physical strength that they need.

Lord, we thank You right now that every caregiver is blessed and strengthened wherever they are weak. We thank You that they are strengthened to help and to serve well.

We ask that every place of anxiety and every place of fear be conquered and dismantled. We pray that they will not move in fear or anxiety. Father, we ask that You bless them, bless them when they come, and bless them when they go. In the mighty name of Jesus, we pray, and we believe. Amen.

A PRAYER FOR FIRST RESPONDERS

Dr. Kwesi Kamau

God, we thank You for the opportunity to come into Your presence. We come before you on behalf of first responders. They are protectors and those who risk their lives to help others. They have so much to deal with in their bodies, souls, and spirits. They struggle with trauma and depression. They face their own physical healing, often because of stress and job-related injuries. We ask for Your healing. We pray that they may see Your hand, hear Your voice, and feel Your presence. Be a God of comfort, consolation, strength, and provision for them in a powerful way.

Lord, they are dealing with feelings of loneliness and guilt. Guilt because while others have died, they survived, and they feel guilty for merely living. They're dealing with increasing demands at work. We pray that You would show up with and for them.

Strengthen Your church to support them, to hold up their arms, to surround them, to keep them, to love them, to create a healing circle around them. Speak to us, God, and empower us for the work that You would have us do to take care of and stand with first responders, globally. It's in Jesus' name we pray. Amen.

A PRAYER FOR PARENTS

Pastor Linda Davis

Gracious and everlasting God, our souls honor You. Your power is absolute. We confess Your Word as truth over all parents, young and old, that they will discipline, teach, and train their children with love and patience just as You, oh Lord, discipline, teach, and train those You love.

Help parents not to grow weary or tired, but to trust You to provide the strength and wisdom that they need. We ask that You help parents to be wise about taking care of themselves so that they will be prepared to meet the needs of their children. Show them how to stay consistent in studying Your Word. May they never be too prideful to receive help from others when they need it. Teach them to depend on You to do what they cannot. Open doors of opportunities to help them gain access to resources, information, and equipment that they will need to give quality care to their children. Empower parents with the knowledge and skill to structure a life that will compel their children to honor and obey You as their God. Father God, help parents do all that You have called us to do.

Remind every parent, Lord, to trust You with all of their hearts. Help us to lean not unto our own understanding but rather acknowledge You in all our ways. Teach parents to be still and to wait on You. It's in the precious, powerful, and mighty name of Jesus the Christ we do pray. Let us say, Amen.

A PRAYER FOR LAW ENFORCEMENT

Rev. Andrā Johnson

Father, we thank You for who You are. We know that You are omnipotent, omniscient, and omnipresent; thus, we bring before You law enforcement agencies, knowing the issues they go through. We're asking for Your guidance so that they will see things the way You do.

We pray that You will fill them with Your Spirit so that they will make decisions that will bring glory to Your name, instead of human decisions that bring fear. We know that law enforcement officers are human beings, and they, too, experience fear. But we're praying that they see people as You do, as they operate with those they made an oath to serve and protect.

We pray that You protect police officers. We pray for their protection, knowing that they have a dangerous job, and we know that they're putting themselves into dangerous and questionable situations. We're praying for their empathy and for their sympathy, and that they receive the same.

We're praying that they will love like You love because You said in Your Word that love covers a multitude of sins. Father, send them Your love, send them Your spirit. We pray that Your will be done in every one of their lives. It's in Jesus' name we pray. Amen.

PRAYERS FOR LEGISLATORS

Bishop John D. Ogletree, Jr.

Heavenly Father, we pray that Your kingdom come, Your will be done in our legislative bodies. Let Your will be done in every state, county, and city legislative and governing bodies, and in the U.S. House of Representatives and Senate. Father, You are aware of the polarization that exists in our nation among people and those charged with passing laws and setting budgets. We pray, God, that they recognize what Your Word in Leviticus 24 defines and gives instructions for a system of laws that protects and shows love to all people, not just those of a particular political party, socioeconomic standing, or race. Open the hearts of state and national congressional representatives to understand how the pandemic worsened social, racial, and economic inequities that existed in Black, brown, and poor communities. Help them to see how this has affected mental health in our families. Father, we pray that You would guide governing bodies to address the challenges that profoundly affect citizens nationally, inflation, public school funding, raises for our teachers, gun control, and accessible medical insurance. And finally, God, according to Romans 13, do not allow legislative bodies to be a terror to Your people. Let them fear and serve You and be servants for good. In the name of our Lord and Savior Jesus Christ, we pray. Amen.

Pastor Bryant Phelps

> "God of our weary years. God of our silent tears. God, who has brought us thus far along the way."

Lord, for too long, we have been impacted by and have witnessed the erosion of trust in our elected officials. We have forgotten Your purposeful intentions to be caretakers of creation and have again mistaken our agency as power equal to Yours. Forgive us, we pray, and free us for joyful participation with You. "Lest our feet stray"*, God, we pray for the love, peace, and a sound mind for those elected to serve that they may hear the cry of the needy. Honor the human dignity of all, regardless of race, creed, gender, ability, sexual orientation, or class. Lest their feet stray, might You remind them that they are called to do justice, love mercy, and walk humbly with You and their neighbors. Lest their feet stray, oh, God, trouble them until they seek to bring an end to the triple evils of racism, classism, and militarism.

> "Shadow beneath thy hand,"* God, might we stand together, the elected and unelected, like we are Your people and bound together by Your spirit as sisters and brothers. Now more than ever, we need thy peace, yearn for thy power, and pray for thy hope for such a time as this in the name of Jesus the Christ we pray. Amen.
>
> * (from *Lift Every Voice and Sing*, James Weldon Johnson and John Rosamond Johnson)

PRAYERS FOR COMMUNITY HEALING

Mrs. Margine Mims

Father, we come today thanking You and praising You for all of Your goodness. It's a blessing to come before You, knowing that You have brought us this far. We pray for communities all over the world. There's so much that needs to be done. We praise You for the things that You are doing in our lives and communities, for the things that You are going to do, and for the things that You've already done, God.

You've been faithful to us. In times like these, we need a Savior. We need someone who will come and rescue us. Our communities need You. Our children need You. Our churches need You. Our families need You, God. Stretch out Your mighty hand today and touch every community and community leader. We need Your help. We need You to intervene in our lives today. Intervene in communities today. God, bring us together. Erase division in the name of Jesus, and we will praise and magnify You. We believe and trust You, in Jesus' name. Amen.

Joel Smyer

Dear Lord, we are reminded of the prayer of Nehemiah when he learned that the remnant who survived captivity were in great distress, and that there were broken walls, and so, a broken community. Lord, we come, and we stand in the gap, confessing the sins of our fathers in the United States. While those sins were committed against You, they continue to cause damage and pain to our Black and marginalized communities,

Lord, we are calling on You to ignite believers of every color, every culture, to return to You, Father. And it is not lost on us that we have a great enemy that wants to leverage and cause mayhem and destroy communities through sin. Father, in the name of Jesus, we cast that enemy down and cancel his intentions.

Holy Spirit, use us to help heal broken communities in Jesus' name. Put Your shield around broken communities all across our land. Protect marginalized communities from any further attacks from our enemy. Dismantle racism, covetousness, greed, injustice, and the dismantling of underlying root sins that our enemy takes and manifests in great ways. And Lord, we are so thankful that greater are You in us than he who is in the world. We ask for the blood, the truth, and the power of the gospel to rebuild and heal broken communities.

We have faith, Lord. We ask for revival in our land. We ask for restoration in our land according to Your Scripture. We give You praise and honor in Jesus' name. Amen.

A PRAYER FOR OBEDIENCE TO HIS DIRECTION

The Honorable Judge Cheryl Williams

> "His mother said to the servants, 'Do whatever he tells you.'" ~John 2:5 (NIV)

Jesus' mother knew who Jesus was, and she told the servants to be obedient. Because I know that Jesus is my Lord and Savior, I (we) too must be obedient – to do whatever Jesus tells me (us) to do. Remembering that obedience is better than sacrifice. Today, I will be obedient by praying and waiting to hear from God. And after hearing from God, I will be obedient to His Word. I will seek Him more through prayer so that I have dialogue with Him to hear from God and discern His voice. Lord, thank you for Jesus. Help me to spend quality time each day with You in prayer and in Your Word, so that I can discern Your voice. Lord, help me to be obedient to You and Your Word. Move me out of my way so that I can be obedient to You. Thank you for grace and mercy. It is in Jesus' name, I pray, Amen.

A PRAYER FOR THE NATION

Minister Sonya Hosey

Heavenly Father, we come before You standing in the gap of our nation in this hour of uncertainty, division, and unrest. We turn our eyes back to You, the One who holds all power, all mercy, and justice. Your Word says, "If my people who are called by my name would humble themselves and pray and seek my face and turn from their wicked ways, then I will hear from heaven and I will forgive their sins and will heal their land."

Lord, we humble ourselves, seek Your face, and ask for forgiveness for those who have too often turned away from Your truth. Heal us, so that we may know that this land can be healed from the pain of injustice, from the wounds of division, from the grip of pride, and fear.

Infuse leaders with wisdom, righteousness, compassion, and integrity. Lead them to protect the vulnerable and to serve the people well. Bring Your Spirit into our communities, families, nation, and world. Let revival arise. Let our hearts be softened.

Strengthen the church that we may be a light in darkness. That we will not get weary in well-doing. That we walk boldly in love and truth. We cry out for justice and for mercy.

Bind up the brokenhearted, comfort the grieving, protect the children, awaken the consciousness of the world. You alone are our hope. Father God, we say thank You for what You're doing in this time, in this season. We pray in Jesus Christ's name, our Redeemer and our King. Amen.

A PRAYER FOR FAMILIES AND COMMUNITIES

Rosalind Rayford

Father God, we come to You humble, empty, and in full submission; our hearts filled with prayer for peace, reconciliation, and stability within our homes. Because You are the foundation of love and the source of healing, and the corrector of all things broken, we believe it to be done in the name of Jesus. We humbly ask that You bring unity where division is present. Provide us understanding where discourse has consumed us, and compassion where hearts have been broken and hardened. We pray for restoration because peace is in jeopardy.

God, we ask that You heal the wounds and trauma of the past. Restore forgiveness for those who are vulnerable and have been violated. Restore bitterness with grace, resentment with forgiveness, and sadness with joy. God, allow Your presence to reside daily within each of us and in each home. Lord, guide our conversations and strengthen relationships. Confirm the necessity of Your men, Lord. Heal all fractured relationships between spouses, parents, and children, so that families will be whole again. God, we pray that every household be a sanctuary of peace in Your name.

God, we surrender to Your wisdom and grace, trusting that You will bring healing and restoration in Your perfect time. You are the Alpha and Omega of our faith. God, we pray all these things in Jesus' name, Amen.

A PRAYER FOR TIMES OF CRISIS & SUFFERING

Pastor Mosely Hobson

Father, in the name of Jesus, help us to stand on Your Word in the time of crisis and suffering. Help us to believe that even though it seems like the answers are not coming, nor is Your hand moving fast enough, that You're going to deliver according to Your Word. We seek Your face today. We pray that we will wait upon the Lord to renew our strength. Father, we lean on Your Word. When it seems like the winds of life are blowing, that we are moving and bending, help us to be like that tree that's planted by the river.

God, You delivered the children of Israel, and we know that You will deliver us. When we don't know what to do, when we don't know how to move, when we don't know what to believe, help us not only to stand on You, but also to lean on one another. Help us not to isolate ourselves, but to draw close to those who are in faith with us. Thank You for calling Your church to the forefront, that we might be that beacon of hope, that we might be that light that represents You. That even when governments and others fail us, You never will. You are a very present help.

And for that, we say thank You, we honor You, and we bless You for giving us resilience. We thank You for it all. In Jesus' name. Amen.

A PRAYER FOR GLOBAL PEACE AND STABILITY

Carolotta Forester-Langford

Father God, we thank You today that the peace that we have is the peace that comes from You. We thank You right now that You are the blessed hope that we have.

Lord, we know that there is devastation all over the world. We know that there are rumors of war, and there are wars. We ask where there is devastation, that You release peace. Our land is being terrorized. Our land is being destroyed. But You are the Maker of all land. You are the Keeper of the land. And, Lord, we thank You right now for giving us peace despite how the land is being taken for granted.

God, we ask that You give us peace in the midst of the storm. Grant each of us inner peace because of who You are. Give us peace in our minds, in our homes, in our churches, in our well-being. We thank You for the full armor of God. We put on the mantle of peace and stability. God, in Your sufficiency, give us stability of thought, emotion, and reason. We find strength in Your abilities. Despite what we see, we know You make all things well.

God, it is well despite what we see. You are our Comforter. You are our peace. You are our banner. We declare peace over every hardship around us and in us. In Jesus' mighty name we pray. Amen.

A PRAYER FOR JUSTICE & RIGHTEOUSNESS

Shree Moffett

Father, we come to You by faith in Jesus' name. We declare Your Word over injustice and unrighteousness. Your Word declares that You will establish Your throne, and only Your throne will be built with justice and righteousness. We thank You for the establishment of Your throne in this world.

Lord God, that You promised that Your Word would accomplish what You sent it to do. We know then that Your Word is bringing healing to classism, racism, and injustice. We thank You that our churches are beacons of light, that our church is a city set on a hill, that we are the salt of the world, we're even the light that You call us to be in our communities. Father, we call on You, and we thank You for the healing coming to this world.

We bind the hand of the enemy that wants to continue to bring division, strife, and contention. We loose healing, hope, justice, and righteousness in the earth, in our communities, and in our families.

Lord, You alone get glory. We look to You, the author and finisher of our faith. We expect to see what we're praying for. We expect to see justice and righteousness. We expect to see our communities healed and unified.

We thank You that it is so. We put our faith in agreement with You. And Your Word is declared, so we give You thanks for today. In the name of Jesus. Amen.

A PRAYER FOR THE ECONOMY & WORKFORCE

Pastor Michael Mason

God, we come before You to thank You for Your Word declares that we have the victory. We pray that You would bless the economy. Father, we pray for those who are going through difficult times, those who are dealing with challenging situations, and those who have lost their jobs. We pray for families who are struggling. We ask that You meet every need.

We pray for peace in homes and on the job. Father, we ask that You turn economic systems around. Turn them around, God, because we are claiming victory. You said in Your Word, we are more than conquerors, and that we can do all things through Christ who strengthens us. Father, we thank You that the peace of God is ruling in our lives, and we call upon Your name, God, to bless this nation and to bless this economy.

We thank You even though the financial struggles don't seem fair. We still trust You to turn it around. In Jesus' name, Amen.

A PRAYER FOR MENTAL & EMOTIONAL WELL-BEING

Pastor Daryl Horton

Dear Lord, we call upon Your holy and righteous name, asking that You would be with those struggling with anxiety, challenged with depression, or struggling with trauma. We come praying for healing and asking that You would bring peace to their minds and lives.

Be with those who are challenged with issues like dementia or Alzheimer's. Bring healing and deliverance to all who are challenged by factors impacting their mental, psychological, and emotional well-being.

Your Word declares unto us that we should have the same mind that is in Christ Jesus. So, we ask that You help us to defeat those things that come against us and challenge our minds. We ask that You restore the memory of those to whom it has been lost.

God, cover our minds, protect us, heal us, and redeem us. God, thank You for counselors, clinicians, psychiatrists, and psychologists who use Your Word and the gifts You have placed inside of them to heal Your people. We thank You for their work to help us reduce the stigma in our communities. We ask, God, that You be a glimmer of hope in the lives of those battling mental health conditions, reminding them that You will never leave them nor forsake them.

We ask that You continue to provide resources to Your churches and ministries, to assist people to get the help that they need. We depend on You for healing, for empowerment, and for peace. We pray all of this in the mighty and magnificent name of Your Son, Jesus the Christ. Amen.

A PRAYER FOR THE MILITARY & VETERANS

Pastor Robert Campbell

Almighty God, we come before You with hearts full of gratitude and reverence to honor the brave soldiers who have served our nation. Those who stood in the gap previously, and active military personnel who continue to do so. They bore and bear burdens so that others may live in freedom and peace. Continue to bless them, to strengthen them, and to give them peace. In a world filled with uncertainty, we are reminded that Your promises remain steadfast. Just as an anchor holds firm against the winds and the waves, Your love holds us steady through the storms of life. Lord, we ask You to pour out Your comfort upon active military and veterans who are hurting. Pour out Your guidance when they are suffering, Your peace when they are weary, and Your protection while they are serving.

For every veteran who still carries their visible wounds of service, let them know they are never forgotten, and they are never alone. Lord, wrap them in Your arms and remind them that You are their hope. We ask that You heal them and restore them. For every active military personnel, likewise, remind them that You are their hope. Though battles may rage around them, remind them You are their shield.

Unite us in purpose and love, as we pray for armed forces stationed around the world, and those who are now veterans. We pray that they will be blessed in a mighty way. Now, Lord, according to Your will, bless us and keep us in Jesus' name. We ask this all, believing that it is already done. Amen.

PRAYERS FOR THE VULNERABLE AND THE OPPRESSED

Pastor Marvin Walker

Gracious God, we thank You for being God, all by Yourself. We beseech your mercy for the vulnerable and the oppressed. We pray that You hear our cry on their behalf. The widows, the orphans, those who were oppressed, suppressed, and are in vulnerable states. Lord, would You be their help and be their portion? The psalmist wrote that you will not only spare the poor, but You will deliver them.

We thank You for this kind of redemption that only You can give. Jesus, we're thankful that You're able to remove them from every type of oppression that leaves them vulnerable and open to the attack of the enemy. Their lives are precious in Your sight. Lord, we're asking that You meet folks who are in the midst of hard, hurting situations, and You be the God of all comfort. God, use us to see, reach, speak, lead, love, engage, pray for, and look at every individual that is in a vulnerable or oppressed situation, to be Your hands and feet. Give us the heart, eyes, and ears to help us meet needs as Your servants in a humble manner. In Jesus' name we pray. Amen.

Pastor Emma Alexander

Almighty God, we thank You for the blessings of this day. God, please help us make this world a better place as we serve others in true solidarity, seeking to find ways to help the poor, the marginalized, and those who are suffering, and to always seek to work towards the greater good. We know that we cannot do anything without Your guidance, or without Your divine hands to inspire us, lead us, and give us Your wisdom. We can do all things throughout this day and the days, months, and years ahead, because of you.

May Your grace be ever present with us. We seek Your strength, and we ask Your Holy Spirit to guide us in our decisions. God of love, teach us to give our best, to speak with love, to act with courage. Teach us to use Your time wisely and with intentionality. May we be good stewards of all the gifts You have given us. In the name of the Incarnate Word, we pray. Amen.

A PRAYER FOR THE PERSECUTED CHURCH

Elder Leon Parker

Dear gracious, kind Father, in the name of Jesus, we come before You, on behalf of our persecuted brothers and sisters around the world. You see their suffering, their sacrifice, their unwavering faith. Strengthen them through the power of the Holy Ghost. Let Your spirit comfort them. Let Your angels encamp around about them. Your Word declares in Second Timothy 3:12 (KJV), "Yea, and all that will live godly in Christ Jesus shall suffer persecution." But we know that You are faithful to keep them through every trial. Let their boldness shake the gates of hell.

Let miracles and deliverance confirm their witness, and even in secret places, let revival break forth. Lord, our hope is anchored in You. You are the Author and Finisher of our faith. We believe that even in suffering, Your glory will be revealed. Let the persecuted church hold fast to the blessed hope of Your return, knowing that victory is already won.

We plead the blood of Jesus over the persecuted church. No weapon shall form against them, nor those that might form shall prosper. We declare victory, strength, and endurance in Jesus' name. Amen.

A PRAYER FOR THE NEXT GENERATION

Comfort Brown

Dear Heavenly Father, we lift the next generation to You. You alone are our blessed hope, and I pray that You would be the firm foundation upon which they stand. May they find their confidence, strength, and future in You.

Lord, be the source of their hope, the One who leads them into the promise of a brighter tomorrow for all who place their trust in You. Let Your mercy and grace go before them. Cover them with Your protection and make their paths straight.

Jesus, we ask that You guard their hearts and minds. Do not let the enemy sift them like wheat. As Psalm 140 declares, do not grant the wicked desires; let not their plans succeed.

Thank You, Lord, that You know the plans You have for this generation, plans to prosper them and not to harm them, plans to give them hope and a future (Jeremiah 29:11). You are faithful through all generations, and we trust in Your unfailing love.

We ask all these blessings over the next generation, in the mighty and matchless name of Jesus, Amen.

A PRAYER TO BREATHE LIFE INTO OUR COMMUNITIES, NATION, AND THE WORLD

Sherrye Ellison Willis

Father, we humbly come into Your presence with gratitude, surrendering all to You. Create in us clean hearts and renew right spirits within us. We repent of every sin and receive the forgiveness Jesus died to give us. We come asking for a release of Your holy breath of revival upon the nations. Your word declares in Job 34:14 -15 that if You were to withdraw Your spirit and Your breath, humanity would cease to exist. We intercede for the nations and cry out: breathe on us again.

Let Your kingdom rule in our lives, homes, and communities. Let a fresh breath of life flow into weary hearts laboring for justice. Let the wind of revival sweep across nations. Direct us, guide us, and let Your will be done. Strengthen us to stand firm in

Your grace and preserve our well-being so that we may flourish where You have planted us. Grant wisdom to our leaders. Give them divine strategies to repair broken systems and grace to face the challenges.

We thank You for the provision flooding our communities. Food, clothing for the poor, safe shelter, meaningful work, training opportunities, and strategies to help restore dignity and stability. Where resources are scarce, release abundance.

You cause all things to work together for our good. Thank You that we will see renewal and restoration in our communities. We surrender every worry into Your hands. We praise You now for the outcome because victory has already been declared in the name of Jesus Christ, our Lord. Amen.

THE GIFT OF PRAYER BOOK CONTRIBUTORS

Pastor Emma Alexander
True Vine Church

Minister Leonard Allen
Praise Cathedral Church of God In Christ

Grayland Barrett

Comfort Brown
Alliance for Greater Works

Madison Brown

Pastor Robert Campbell
Point of Grace Church

Vicky Coffee

Pastor Linda Davis
Boynton Chapel United Methodist Church

Carolotta Forester-Langford
Liberty Grace Community Church

Jacob Garcia

Kierston Harris

Pastor Mosely Hobson
Greater St. Johns Church of God In Christ

Dr. Erica Holmes
HOMMs Consulting

Pastor Daryl Horton
Mt. Zion Baptist Church

Minister Sonya Hosey
Abundant Life Church

Jeff Howard

Vivian Jackson

Pastor Anita Jahwar
Kingdom Worship and Restoration Church

Rev. Andrā Johnson

Jada Jones

K. Graham

Dr. Kwesi Kamau
Impact Church DFW

Lanai Johnson

Elder Melvin Lee
Refiner's Fire Rhema Ministries

LaLoni Leffall

Pastor Michael Mason
Manasseh Church

Pastor Tonya McGill
Antioch Christian Church

Dr. Cynthia McKnight
Revolving Hearts Ministries

Mrs. Margine Mims
Morris County Collaborative

Shree Moffett
LightChurch

Pastor Annie Nelson
Disciples of Faith Worship Center

Bishop John D. Ogletree, Jr.
First Metropolitan Church

Elder Leon Parker
Zion Apostolic Temple

Pastor Vincent Parker
Golden Gate Missionary Baptist Church

Dr. Sheron Patterson

Pastor Bryant Phelps
Hamilton Park United Methodist Church

Dr. Maurice Pugh
New Life Fellowship

Rosalind Rayford
Four Winds Bible Church

Brandon Sanders

Joel Smyer

Elaine Sommerville, CPA

Frank Sommerville, JD, CPA

Bryce Timm

Brennan Timm

Rylee Vlaun-Wright

Pastor Marvin Walker
Watermark Community Church

Dr. Ricky Walter
Lifeline Children and Family Services

Dr. David Wang
Fuller Theological Seminary

The Honorable Judge Cheryl Williams

Sherrye Ellison Willis
Alliance for Greater Works

SPECIAL THANKS

Alliance for Greater Works' Board of Directors
- **The Honorable Judge Cheryl Williams**, Chairperson
- **Euralonda Baptist Gates**
- **Cassandra Greenfield**, The Greenfield Group, Corp
- **Mark Hays**, Tulsa Community Center
- **Alphonso Jackson**, CPA
- **Dr. Elizabeth Moffitt**, The Christopher Quinn Group, Inc.
- **Satrina Reid**
- **Terez Smith**, CPA
- **Dr. Ricky Walter**, Lifeline Children & Family Services, Inc.

Alliance for Greater Works' Resilient Church Collective Steering Committee
- **Dr. Chris Adams**, Biola University
- **Dr. Eric Brown**, Boston University
- **Vicky Coffee**
- **Dr. Christin Fort**, Fuller Theological Seminary
- **Dr. Erica Holmes**, HOMMs Consulting
- **Dr. Blaire Lewis**, Battlefield Global Ministries
- **Dr. David Wang**, Fuller Theological Seminary

Dr. Cynthia Rembert James, Landmark Ministries & Protege

Lilly Endowment, Inc.

2022-2025 Resilient Church Collective Cohorts

All our partners and friends who made this project possible

Book published with a grant from:

www.ingramcontent.com/pod-product-compliance
Lightning Source LLC
Chambersburg PA
CBHW072003060526
44107CB00149B/185